2u

kids' he

worcestershire
countycouncil
Libraries & Learning

D0332422

Cara Hobday

kids' healthy lunchbox

Over 50 delicious and nutritious recipes for children of all ages

hamlyn

Note:

Both metric and imperial measurements are given for the recipes. Use one set of measures only, not a mixture of both.

Ovens should be preheated to the specified temperature. If using a fan-assisted oven, follow the manufacturer's instructions for adjusting the time and temperature. Grills should also be preheated.

This book includes dishes made with nuts and nut derivatives. It is advisable for those with known allergic reactions to nuts and nut derivatives and those who may be potentially vulnerable to these allergies, such as pregnant and nursing mothers, invalids, the elderly and babies, to avoid dishes made with nuts and nut oils. It is also prudent to check the labels of preprepared ingredients for the possible inclusion of nut derivatives.

The Department of Health advises that eggs should not be consumed raw. This book contains some dishes made with raw or lightly cooked eggs. It is prudent for more vulnerable people such as pregnant and nursing mothers, invalids, the elderly, babies and young children to avoid uncooked or lightly cooked dishes made with eggs.

Meat and poultry should be cooked thoroughly. To test if poultry is cooked, pierce the flesh through the thickest part with a skewer or fork – the juices should run clear, never pink or red.

Portion sizes are average adult portions, so you will need to adjust them according to the appetite and age of your child.

First published in Great Britain in 2007 by
Hamlyn, a division of Octopus Publishing Group Ltd
2–4 Heron Quays, London E14 4JP

ISBN-13: 978-0-600-61581-1
ISBN-10: 0-600-61581-2

A CIP catalogue record for this book is available from the British Library

Printed and bound in China

10 9 8 7 6 5 4 3 2 1

Contents

Introduction

Healthy lunches, happy kids

Any parent's ultimate goal must be to produce a happy and fulfilled child. But how do you achieve that ideal state? Having a child who is happy at school, enjoying packed and energetic, yet predictable, days, and reaching their full potential is difficult to guarantee and depends on many different factors, some of which you, as a parent, cannot influence.

What you can influence, however, is your child's diet by providing him or her with a healthy lunchbox. Children need the right foods to keep them going through the day so that they can carry out their tasks of learning and playing and growing. Healthy food will give them enough energy to last the day and will also provide the building blocks for a healthy adult.

In this book you will find the recipes you need for this kind of diet. You will find lunches for when children need extra brainpower, for growth spurt times, for when they need to pack a lot of the good stuff into a small lunchbox and for when they need lots of energy to chase a ball around the playground all lunch hour and then swim lengths of a pool all afternoon. And all these lunchbox ideas are so delicious and appealing that children won't realize just how healthy they are.

The food in lunchboxes is out of the refrigerator for up to six hours before being eaten, and on a hot summer's day it may well become quite warm, which could lead to food poisoning where meats and fish are concerned. Starting with food that comes straight from the refrigerator, or was prepared and then refrigerated, is a good idea, as is packing a small frozen ice pack in with the food. Encourage your child to leave the lunchbox somewhere cool, if possible.

Note that, due to nut allergies, some schools ban children from having nuts in any form in their lunchboxes. However, the recipes here that contain nuts can simply have the nut element removed and still be delicious.

Taking charge of the lunchbox

The best kind of energy is the kind that is consistent, avoiding the highs and lows provided by sugar. To find this kind of good stuff in the supermarket, you will need to arm yourself against the charms of many food manufacturers and the irresistible appeal of clever packaging (what's inside may not be so clever) and navigate away from the countless 'lunchbox fillers', both savoury and sweet, that are specially designed for busy parents.

The easiest and safest way to know what has gone into your child's lunchbox is to make it yourself; in that way you will know that the calories come from protein and fibre, not surplus-to-requirements fats, sugars and salts.

To really take charge of your child's lunchbox, you have to focus on what your child needs and how the lunchbox can provide it. What they need may not always tie up exactly with what they want, however, so it may take a bit of perseverance to introduce some foods or to change established patterns and get your children enjoying their healthy lunches. (In the face of a negative reaction, don't give up at the first hurdle, simply retreat, regroup and try again another time.)

If you don't already own an electric hand mixer, hand blender or food processor, consider investing in one now, as these will help you make cakes, pastries and soups for healthy lunches. You will also need a good supply of airtight plastic containers in a range of sizes. Buy cheap ones and use them in a semi-disposable manner or go for better quality ones, which will last a lot longer, especially if they go through the dishwasher regularly.

Choosing healthy foods

It is easy to get enough calories into a packed lunch, but the much harder job is to get the right

kind of calories into them to make your child stay aware until the end of the day, without the typical highs and lows that a sugar and additive-heavy lunch can provide. This is where you have to be on your toes as a lunchbox packer – and make the right choices.

Choose sunflower or olive oil margarine as a spread rather than butter; choose wholegrain white bread instead of white bread; choose water instead of a sugar-packed carton of fruit drink – all these little changes add up to a big difference in the healthy balance of a lunchbox. Go further by adding a bit of lettuce to a ham sandwich, changing to a low-fat mayonnaise and adding a handful of seeds to a salad or your baking.

Enjoy guilt-free cakes and biscuits simply by making your own. Many commercial cakes and biscuits have hydrogenated fat as a preservative, though most supermarkets no longer sell these, and a high sugar and salt content that only the most indulgent of home-made cakes could match. Hydrogenated fats, or trans fats, are fats that our bodies cannot process and will still be with your child 40 years from now. Simple eggs, butter, flour and sugar score lots of points on the nutrition scale, too.

If you make your own pastry (which is easy to do if you own a food processor), nutrients can be added here too. I usually replace a bit of plain flour with wholemeal, and you can also add seeds such as in the homemade sausage rolls (see page 54), and omit the salt, if desired, in most recipes. Making pastry in large batches and freezing what you don't immediately need means you'll have some to hand when you need it.

Dangerous salt

Many people in the western world eat much more salt than is recommended for a healthy diet. It is important to realize that about three-quarters of our intake now comes from salt added to processed food. Children over 11 years are recommended to have an intake of no more than 6 g per day, children of 7–10 years old are recommended 5 g per day and children of 4–6 years old are recommended just 3 g per day. So, if a child has sugar-coated cornflakes for breakfast (1.5 g), a cheese or ham breadsticks lunch pack for lunch (2.4 g) and chicken nuggets for tea (1.75 g), that, at nearly twice his or her recommended salt intake, is a recipe for a stroke in later life.

High salt intake is a major cause of high blood pressure, heart disease and strokes. Too much salt in the diet is therefore harmful. It also plays a role in gastric cancer and osteoporosis. It is much more hazardous than sugar because, although sugar affects your teeth and your weight, salt affects your basic health and constitution. Simply by checking the labels you can make yourself aware of salt levels and ensure your child gets the right building blocks for a healthy life.

Forward planning

Before you even go into the kitchen, you need to go shopping, and before you go shopping, you need a plan. I find it a huge help to plan our week's eating in advance – it means I can plan the shopping, I can use up leftovers and everybody gets their turn at their favourites. When you know what you will be putting in packed lunches every day, you don't have the morning 'What's for lunch?' dilemma.

Begin by making a list of foods that your children will eat, including all their favourites of course, and then add those foods that you would like them to eat and that they are happy to try. You will probably be surprised at how long the list is. Then simply plan the weeks accordingly.

I suggest that you plan your packed lunches menu by looking through this book with your child(ren) and making a list of their favourites and your favourites. Then it is simply a case of filling in the weekly lists, allowing for leftovers, club nights (which might require a more substantial lunch), after-school activities, etc. On pages 10–11 I have made up a sample month's plan, where there are two after-school clubs per week, and one child having packed lunch.

Monthly lunch plan

WEEK ONE

Monday
Turkey, Bacon and Bean Salad, piece of fruit, Apple and Berry Turnover

Tuesday
Sardines on Rye, cucumber and tomato, Melon and Pineapple Salad (After-school snack: toasted seeds – see page 12)

Wednesday
Spanish Tortilla, Cheddar cheese sticks, Fruit Skewers with Yogurt Dip

Thursday
Turkey, Bacon and Bean Salad, Melon and Pineapple Salad, toasted seeds (see page 12) (After-school snack: 2 Oaty Banana Mini Muffins)

Friday
Sardines on Rye, Apple and Berry Turnover

WEEK TWO

Monday
Tuna Pâté Crispbreads, cucumber and tomato, Fruit Shortbread

Tuesday
Fruity Coleslaw, piece of fruit, Fruit Shortbread (After-school snack: Rice cakes with yeast extract spread and cottage cheese)

Wednesday
Tuna Pâté Crispbreads, Malted Chocolate Milk, piece of fruit

Thursday
Sweet Potato and Ham Burgers, red pepper sticks, Fruit Skewers with Yogurt Dip (After-school snack: 2 Oaty Banana Mini Muffins)

Friday
Fruity Coleslaw, cucumber and tomato, Apple and Berry Turnover

WEEK THREE

Monday
Tuna Quesadilla, cucumber and tomato, Apple and Berry Turnover

Tuesday
Tuna and Tomato Pasties (1–2, depending on age of child), piece of fruit, 2 slices of Orange Tea Loaf spread with butter and sandwiched together (After-school snack: piece of Date and Apple Muesli Slice)

Wednesday
Prawns with Fruity Salad, cucumber and tomato, Fruit Smoothie

Thursday
All-day Breakfast Sandwich, piece of fruit, Apple and Berry Turnovers (After-school snack: piece of Date and Apple Muesli Slice)

Friday
Tuna and Tomato Pasties, Fruit Skewers with Yogurt Dip, slice of Choc-peanut Cake

WEEK FOUR

Monday
Haloumi and Pasta Salad, piece of fruit, 2 slices of Orange Tea Loaf spread with butter and sandwiched together

Tuesday
Chinese-style Turkey Wraps, cucumber and tomato, 2 Maple Syrup Flapjacks (After-school snack: 2 Oaty Banana Mini Muffins)

Wednesday
Haloumi and Pasta Salad, cucumber and tomato, 2 Maple Syrup Flapjacks

Thursday
Chinese-style Turkey Wraps, piece of fruit, toasted seeds (After-school snack: 2 slices of Orange Tea Loaf spread with butter and sandwiched together)

Friday
Honey-salmon and Potato Salad, piece of fruit, Malted Chocolate Milk

What to buy

When you have a monthly plan in place, shopping is easy, especially if you keep your kitchen well stocked with staples.

Cornerstones of the storecupboard

- Porridge oats
- Seeds: sunflower, pumpkin and linseed, which can be mixed together and roasted for 15 minutes at 180°C (350°F), Gas Mark 4, to make a health-packed snack
- Canned tuna in brine for pâtés, salads or fillings
- White plain flour
- Wholemeal plain flour
- Eggs
- Golden caster sugar (less refined than caster) or soft light brown sugar
- Dried fruit – good for snacks, or for stirring through salads and baking to add extra nutrition-packed calories
- Potatoes
- Onions

Essentials

- Apples – get your child to choose his or her favourite kind from the huge variety on offer
- Cucumber and tomatoes – kids love the newly available small cucumbers, which can be eaten like fruit
- Meat from the deli counter sliced wafer thin
- Frozen berries, either individual fruits, such as raspberries or strawberries, or berry mixes
- Sunflower margarine
- Unsalted butter
- Edam or Gouda cheese – lower in fat than other cheeses, easily grated or can simply be cut into pieces for cheese sticks
- Fresh strawberries and cherries – compare the price of these healthy treats with overpackaged processed food and you will be pleasantly surprised

Occasional snacks

- Crisps – look for low-salt and low-fat varieties of crisps and cheesy biscuits, but still keep them for end-of-term treats
- Tubes of fruit-flavoured fromage frais – yes, they are overpackaged, but the contents are healthy and not processed and young children love them
- Cakes and biscuits – check the labels for hydrogenated fats

SHOPPING LIST

This is an example of a weekly lunchbox shopping list covering the first week of the monthly plan on pages 10–11, including enough food for the Monday of the second week.

Greengrocer/supermarket

- 100 g (3½ oz) broccoli
- 500 g (1 lb) waxy potatoes
- 2 onions
- 1 carrot
- 1 garlic bulb
- 2 red peppers
- 1 bunch of spring onions
- 1 cucumber
- 250 g (8 oz) cherry tomatoes
- 1 round lettuce
- 1 cantaloupe melon
- 1 small pineapple
- 1 lime
- 5 dessert apples
- 125 g (4 oz) seedless grapes
- 125 g (4 oz) strawberries
- 2 medium, ripe bananas
- 1 lemon

Butcher

- 100 g (3½ oz) streaky bacon
- 150 g (5 oz) turkey breast

Grocer/supermarket

- 400 g (13 oz) can mixed beans or kidney beans
- 250 g (8 oz) can sardines in oil
- 75 g (3 oz) can tuna chunks in brine
- canned no-sugar, no-salt sweetcorn
- 425 g (14 oz) can cherries in juice
- rye bread
- rye crispbreads
- corn or sunflower oil
- red wine vinegar
- dijon mustard
- olive oil
- wheatgerm
- almond extract
- fructose
- seeds: sunflower, pumpkin and linseed
- golden caster sugar
- plain flour
- porridge oats
- baking powder
- 12 eggs
- semi-skimmed milk
- 400 g (13 oz) Cheddar or Edam cheese
- 125 g (4 oz) Greek yogurt
- sunflower margarine or butter, for spreading
- 100 g (3½ oz) probiotic yogurt drink – flavour of your choice
- 125 g (4 oz) cream cheese
- 50 g (2 oz) low-fat cream cheese
- 250 g (8 oz) unsalted butter
- 425 g (14 oz) pack frozen ready-rolled puff pastry
- 250 g (8 oz) frozen berries

Sandwich fillings

Bread

The best sandwiches are made with fresh bread. I have suggested fillings in the recipes for a whole range of breads, but whichever bread type you choose, make sure it is fresh. Buy sliced bread and freeze it, and then you can vary the type without having to use it all up. Rolls are also good, although they are better eaten fresh.

There is such a variety of bread available at bakers and supermarkets now that it shouldn't be too difficult to find one that your child likes that also scores points nutritionally. My personal favourite is a bread from a Polish bakery, made from half rye and half wheat flour. It is very versatile, and the kids can't taste the difference between this and normal white wholegrain bread.

Spreads

Sunflower margarine is the best spread, as well as good old butter of course, which may be higher in saturated fats but is free from additives. If you find unsalted butter unpalatable, try a slightly salted one instead, and consider spreadable versions, which can be used straight from the refrigerator. There are also other options – try flavouring the butter or spread with roasted red pepper, for instance, or buy nut butter for extra goodness, such as peanut butter, cashew butter or almond butter.

Fillings

I have not covered the traditional fillings too much, such as egg mayonnaise, chicken mayonnaise, BLT, tuna and sweetcorn or tuna mayonnaise, ham and grated cheese, as I think most people can find their way around these. Many children like pickles and chutneys, which can be partnered with cheese, smoked salmon and, of course, the numerous cold meats available freshly sliced from the deli counter.

Other nutrient-packed fillings

- hummus and alfalfa sprouts
- avocado and sliced turkey
- ham and egg
- taramasalata and cucumber
- pastrami and tomato
- cheese and coleslaw
- peanut butter and grated carrot
- poached or tinned salmon and cucumber
- chicken and guacamole.

Add some crunchy green lettuce or slices of cucumber to any one of these fillings, and the perfect sandwich is complete.

Sandwiches and Wraps

Chinese-style Turkey Wraps

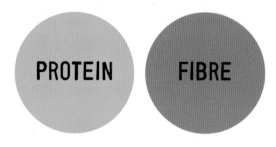

PROTEIN   FIBRE

Ingredients

¹/₂ teaspoon sunflower oil
100 g (3¹/₂ oz) turkey, thinly sliced
1 tablespoon clear honey
2 tablespoons soy sauce
1 tablespoon sesame oil
2 soft flour tortillas
50 g (2 oz) bean sprouts
¹/₄ red pepper, thinly sliced
¹/₄ onion, thinly sliced
25 g (1 oz) mangetouts, sliced
2 baby sweetcorn, thinly sliced

Makes: 2 wraps

Preparation time: 10 minutes

Cooking time: 1–2 minutes

1 Make the filling the evening before. Heat the sunflower oil in a frying pan set over a medium heat and add the turkey to the pan. Stir for 1–2 minutes until cooked through.

2 Reduce the heat and stir in the honey, soy sauce and sesame oil, making sure that the turkey is well coated. Set aside to cool, then put in an airtight container and refrigerate over night.

3 To assemble a wrap, drain the turkey a little and place half the mixture down the centre of the tortilla. Add half the bean sprouts and pepper, onion, mangetouts and baby corn. (Retain the remaining tortilla and mixture for use another day; the mixture will keep for up to 2 days in the refrigerator.)

4 Roll up the tortilla securely and wrap in nonstick baking paper (clingfilm can make the wrap rather soggy).

Turkey and Avocado Focaccia

Avocados are now regarded as a superfood that is very good for brain-power, and turkey is a great sandwich filler – tasty and low in fat.

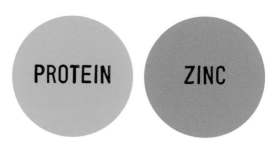

PROTEIN   ZINC

Ingredients

grated rind and juice of 1 lime
25g (1 oz) butter, softened, or sunflower
  margarine
75 g (3 oz) unsmoked bacon, diced
275 g (9 oz) focaccia loaf (enough for four
  sandwiches), quartered and split
1/2 large ripe avocado, sliced
150 g (5 oz) cooked turkey, thinly sliced
1/2 red pepper, thinly sliced
25 g (1 oz) grapes, halved

Makes: 4 sandwiches

Preparation time: 15 minutes

Cooking time: 2 minutes

1 The evening before, mash the grated lime rind and half the lime juice with the butter on a plate.

2 Cook the bacon for around 2 minutes over medium heat (high heat will make it stick) in a dry frying pan, stirring often. Drain on kitchen paper and leave to cool. Refrigerate the lime butter and bacon in separate airtight containers overnight.

3 To assemble the sandwiches, spread the focaccia slices with the lime butter. Sprinkle the avocado with the remaining lime juice. Divide the bacon, turkey and avocado between the sandwiches, top with the red pepper and grapes and wrap securely. (Remaining portions can be kept in the refrigerator for up to 3 days or frozen.)

Salami Ciabatta Rolls

Give salami a healthy balance by having it sliced very finely at the delicatessen (which makes a little look like a lot but still provides plenty of flavour) and including some tasty salad. Note that salami is always better served the same day or the day after slicing.

1 Split the rolls and lightly toast them. Spread lightly with butter.

2 Divide the salami, tomatoes and flat leaf parsley between the rolls. Season with pepper, if using, then wrap securely.

3 Put 2 rolls in the lunchbox and keep the other 2 rolls in the refrigerator for up to 3 days.

Ingredients

4 ciabatta rolls
butter, for spreading
200 g (7 oz) very thinly sliced salami
4 tomatoes, sliced
1 tablespoon chopped flat leaf parsley
freshly ground black pepper (optional)

Makes: 4 rolls

Preparation time: 10 minutes

Cooking time: 2 minutes

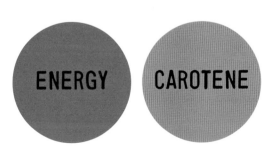

ENERGY   CAROTENE

All-day Breakfast Sandwich

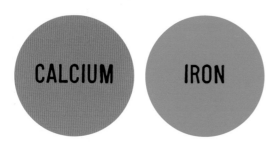

These sandwiches have all the flavour of a cooked breakfast without the unhealthy fats.

Ingredients

3 eggs, beaten
50 ml (2 fl oz) milk
15 g (1/2 oz) butter
125 g (4 oz) button mushrooms, chopped
125 g (4 oz) bacon, diced
4 slices wholemeal bread
tomato ketchup
salt and freshly ground black pepper

Makes: 2 sandwiches

Preparation time: 10 minutes

Cooking time: 12 minutes

1 The evening before, beat together the eggs and milk in a bowl or jug until well combined. Season and set aside.

2 Over a medium heat, melt the butter in a 25 cm (10 inch) nonstick frying pan. Add the mushrooms and stir often. When they are browned all over, which will take about 3 minutes, add the bacon to the pan. Cook for a further 3 minutes until just cooked through but not dry.

3 Spread the bacon and mushroom out evenly across the bottom of the frying pan and pour in the eggs.

4 Cook for 5 minutes, until just cooked through. Stir often with a wooden spoon, gently turning the egg over to cook through. Remove from the pan, set aside to cool, wrap and refrigerate overnight.

5 To assemble the sandwich, spread the bread with the ketchup. Cut the all-day breakfast omelette in 2, cut 1 half to fit the bread and sandwich it between the bread. Keep the remaining half in the refrigerator for up to 3 days.

Tuna Quesadillas

This is one of my personal favourites – it has texture and flavour and the advantage of being healthy too!

Ingredients

4 chapattis or small wholemeal wraps
200 g (7 oz) can tuna in brine, drained
75 g (3 oz) Cheddar or Edam cheese, grated
2 tablespoons chopped white onion
1/2 avocado, thinly sliced
salt and freshly ground black pepper
1 tablespoon oil

Makes: 2 quesadillas

Preparation time: 10 minutes

Cooking time: 12 minutes

FIBRE

PROTEIN

1 The evening before, set out 2 of the chapattis on boards (this will make it easier to slide them into the pan after filling) and divide the tuna between them. Sprinkle over the cheese, onion and avocado. Make sure that the filling is evenly spread. Season lightly and sandwich with the other 2 chapattis.

2 Choose a frying pan that is large enough to hold 1 of the chapatti sandwiches and heat half the oil over a medium-high heat.

3 When the oil is heated, slide the first filled chapatti into the pan and cook for 3 minutes. Use the board to help you turn it by removing the pan from the heat, laying the board over the pan and using an oven glove to turn the quesadilla on to the board. Now slide it back into the pan. Cook for a further 3 minutes on the other side, until golden and the cheese has melted, then slide it out on to a plate. Repeat with the second chapatti.

4 When both chapattis are cool, slice them into quarters. When cold, wrap securely and refrigerate overnight. (If only 1 chapatti is required for lunch, the other portion can be kept in the refrigerator for up to 2 days.)

Tuna Pâté Crispbreads

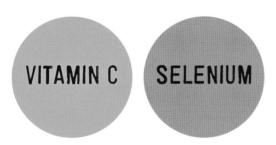

VITAMIN C **SELENIUM**

Ingredients

75 g (3 oz) can tuna chunks in brine, drained
1 teaspoon lemon juice
50 g (2 oz) low-fat cream cheese
1 spring onion, thinly sliced
2 tablespoons canned sweetcorn
8 rye crispbreads
$1/2$ carrot, grated
1 red pepper, thinly sliced
salt and freshly ground black pepper

Makes: 4 sandwiches

Preparation time: 5 minutes

1 Mash the tuna with the lemon juice and cream cheese in a bowl. Adjust the seasoning, then stir in the spring onion and sweetcorn.

2 Assemble 2 sandwiches, using half of the tuna mixture and half of the grated carrot and red pepper. Wrap and place in the lunchbox.

3 Keep the remaining mixture in an airtight container in the refrigerator for up to 3 days.

Tomato-garlic Bread with Ham

This Spanish method of seasoning makes the bread very succulent, and this also means that it needs no butter, so cutting down on the fat.

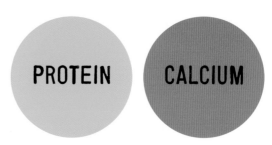

PROTEIN   CALCIUM

Ingredients

1 garlic clove, halved
4 slices from a soft white batch loaf
1 tomato, halved
150g (5 oz) finely sliced ham
75 g (3 oz) Manchego cheese, sliced
1 tomato, finely sliced
salt and freshly ground black pepper

Makes: 2 sandwiches

Preparation time: 10 minutes

Alternative fillings:

Tuna, red pepper and pitted black olives
Sliced hard-boiled egg with sliced onion

1 Rub the cut face of the garlic all over the bread, concentrating on the crusts. Repeat with the tomato halves.

2 Sandwich the bread with the ham, sliced cheese and tomato slices. Season, halve and wrap securely. The remaining sandwich can be kept in the refrigerator for 1 day.

Roasted Vegetable Cornbread

Ingredients

250 g (8 oz) cornmeal or fine polenta
1/2 teaspoon salt
1 teaspoon baking powder
1/2 teaspoon bicarbonate of soda
284 ml (10 fl oz) carton buttermilk
2 eggs, beaten
125 g (4 oz) sunflower margarine, melted
340 g (11 1/2 oz) can red peppers, drained and chopped
4 sun-blush tomatoes, chopped
75 g (3 oz) grilled and marinated aubergines, drained and chopped
1/2 small red onion, finely chopped

Makes: 6 slices

Preparation time: 15 minutes

Cooking time: 45 minutes

IRON   VITAMIN C

1 Line a 500 g (1 lb) loaf tin with nonstick baking paper.

2 In a large bowl, mix together the cornmeal, salt, baking powder and bicarbonate of soda. In a large jug, combine the buttermilk, eggs and melted margarine. Make a well in the centre of the dry ingredients, pour in the egg mixture and then stir until well combined.

3 Stir the chopped vegetables into the mixture until evenly distributed. Pour the mixture into the prepared tin and bake in a preheated oven, 200°C (400°F), Gas Mark 6, for 45–50 minutes until a skewer comes out clean when inserted.

4 Leave to cool in the tin. then turn out on to a wire rack. When cold, wrap securely and refrigerate for up to 3 days. (Alternatively, pre-slice, then freeze.) Serve with cheese sticks if you want to add some protein.

Ham and Cheese Paninis

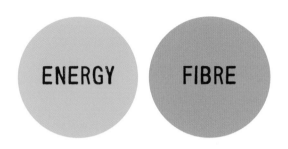

ENERGY   **FIBRE**

Ingredients

1 granary baguette, cut into 2 x 20 cm
  (8 inch) pieces and halved lengthways
butter or sunflower margarine, for spreading
75 g (3 oz) freshly sliced wafer-thin ham
100 g (3½ oz) mild Cheddar cheese, sliced
  thinly with a potato peeler
lettuce leaves
4 cherry tomatoes, sliced
salt and freshly ground black pepper
  (optional)

Makes: 2 paninis

Preparation time: 10 minutes

Cooking time: 10 minutes

1 Place a heavy-based frying pan that is large enough to hold 1 of the paninis over a medium heat.

2 Spread the outside (the crusts) of the halved baguette pieces with the butter or margarine. Divide the ham and cheese between the two baguette sections, season lightly, if desired, and use a fish slice to press the 2 halves together, flattening them slightly.

3 Cook the paninis one at a time in the preheated pan until they are golden on the outside and the cheese has melted. Do not be tempted to increase the heat too much, as the bread will burn before the cheese melts.

4 Set aside to cool completely then wrap securely and refrigerate overnight.

5 To complete, add the lettuce and tomato on the day the panini is to be eaten.

Beef and Asparagus Bagels

If fresh asparagus is unavailable, asparagus, both white and green, in jars is a good substitute, or, failing that, canned asparagus.

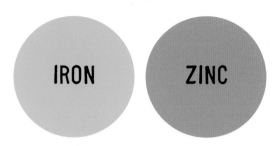

Ingredients

4 asparagus spears, cut into 3
40 g (1½ oz) watercress
1 tablespoon low-fat mayonnaise
1 teaspoon Dijon mustard (optional)
2 multigrain bagels
100 g (3½ oz) cooked beef,
  very thinly sliced
salt and freshly ground black pepper

Makes: 2 bagels

Preparation time: 5 minutes

Cooking time: 5 minutes

1 Put a pan of salted water on to boil. Boil the fresh asparagus briefly, for 30 seconds or so, then drain well and set aside. (Asparagus in jars does not need cooking.)

2 Remove the larger stalks from the watercress and chop it. Place the mayonnaise and mustard, if using, in a bowl and stir in the watercress.

3 Preheat the grill. Split the bagels in half and toast under the grill. Spread the halves with the flavoured mayonnaise. Top with the beef and asparagus spears and wrap securely. (The remaining bagel can be refrigerated for 1–2 days.)

Lamb and Tabbouleh Pittas

This is a tasty way to use up Sunday lunch leftovers. Always slice cooked meat as thinly as possible for more enjoyable sandwiches.

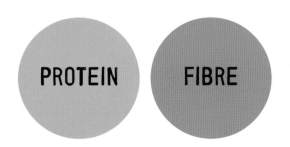

Ingredients

100 g (3½ oz) couscous
100 ml (3½ fl oz) boiling water
2 tablespoons hummus
3 tablespoons olive oil
1 teaspoon lemon juice
1 tablespoon finely chopped mint (optional)
2 tablespoons chopped flat leaf parsley
1 tomato, finely chopped
1 spring onion, finely chopped
25 g (1 oz) cucumber, chopped
125 g (4 oz) cold cooked lamb,
   very thinly sliced
4 wholemeal pittas
salt and freshly ground black pepper

Makes: 4 pittas

Preparation time: 10 minutes

Cooking time: 5 minutes

1 The evening before, place the couscous in a bowl, pour the boiling water over it and leave to soak for 5 minutes. Set aside to cool.

2 Mix together the hummus, oil and lemon juice in a small bowl or jug to make the dressing, adding the mint, if using. Depending on the thickness of the hummus, you may need to add a little water.

3 Stir the parsley, tomato, spring onion and cucumber into the couscous and season lightly. Refrigerate the dressing and tabbouleh overnight in separate airtight containers.

4 To complete the stuffed pittas, split each pitta bread on the day it is needed and toast lightly. Stuff with a quarter of the tabbouleh, top with a quarter of the sliced lamb and spoon over a quarter of the dressing. Wrap securely. (The remaining mixture will keep in the refrigerator for up to 3 days.)

Sardines on Rye

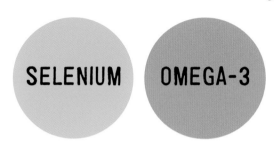

SELENIUM   OMEGA-3

Ingredients

250 g (8 oz) can sardines in oil, drained
125 g (4 oz) cream cheese
2 tablespoons grated cucumber, drained
1 spring onion, finely chopped
6 thin slices of rye bread
sunflower margarine, for spreading
leaves from a round lettuce

Makes: 3 sandwiches

Preparation time: 5 minutes

1 The evening before, drain the sardines, place them in a bowl with the cream cheese and mash them together. Stir in the cucumber and spring onion. Refrigerate in an airtight container overnight.

2 To assemble the sandwiches, spread 3 slices of the rye bread with butter, add the sardine mixture and lettuce and top with the remaining bread. Wrap securely.

3 Use 1 sandwich for the lunchbox and keep the remaining 2 in the refrigerator for up to 3 days.

Salads

Fruity Coleslaw

This comes in the category of great salads, containing foods for brainpower, raw energy, growth building blocks and slow-release sugars. The addition of nuts and raisins makes this coleslaw a complete lunch.

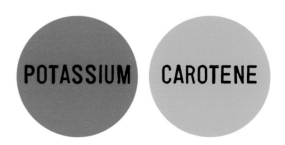

Ingredients

100 g (3¹/₂ oz) white cabbage, shredded
1 carrot, grated
100 g (3¹/₂ oz) pecans, toasted and chopped
2 tablespoons dried cranberries
2 tablespoons raisins
2 sharp dessert apples, diced
2 tablespoons low-fat mayonnaise
salt and freshly ground black pepper

Serves: 2

Preparation time: 15 minutes

Cooking time: 5 minutes

1 Divide the prepared white cabbage, carrot, pecans, cranberries and raisins between 2 airtight containers.

2 Stir in the apple and mayonnaise and check the seasoning. (If you want some coleslaw for another day, do not dress this portion until the day of eating; the undressed coleslaw will keep for up to 3 days in an airtight container in the refrigerator.)

Haloumi and Pasta Salad

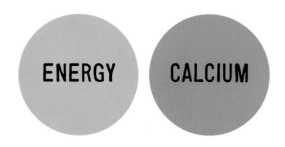

ENERGY   **CALCIUM**

Ingredients

200 g (7 oz) conchiglie pasta
3 tablespoons olive oil
250 g (8 oz) pack marinated haloumi cheese,
   cut into 5 mm (¼ inch) wide slices
3 tablespoons tomato salsa dip
½ x 340 g (11½ oz) can red peppers,
   drained and chopped
2 courgettes, diced
75 g (3 oz) green beans, chopped
salt and freshly ground black pepper

Serves: 4

Preparation time: 15 minutes

Cooking time: 10 minutes

1 The evening before, bring a large saucepan of salted water to the boil and cook the pasta according to the packet instructions. Drain and rinse under the cold tap to cool down. Drain again.

2 Meanwhile, heat 1 tablespoon of the olive oil in a large frying pan over a medium-high heat. Have ready some kitchen paper to drain the cheese on. When the oil is hot enough for the surface to be shimmering (if it is not hot enough, the cheese will simply melt instead of cooking), add the sliced haloumi and cook for 1 or 2 minutes on each side until the cheese is golden. Remove and drain on the kitchen paper. Set aside to cool.

3 In a large bowl, mix together the remaining oil and the tomato salsa dip and add the pepper, courgettes and green beans. Stir in the pasta.

4 Serve the pasta with the cheese (chopped and stirred into the salad, if desired). The seasoning in the salsa dip and the salt from the cheese should be enough for this dish, but adjust to taste if necessary.

5 Enjoy 3 portions for dinner and pack the fourth into an airtight container and refrigerate overnight.

Turkey, Bacon and Bean Salad

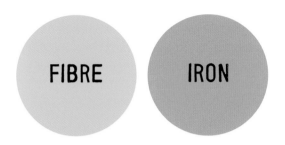

FIBRE

IRON

Ingredients

4 tablespoons sunflower oil
100 g (3½ oz) streaky bacon
150 g (5 oz) turkey breast
1 tablespoon red wine vinegar
1 tablespoon Dijon mustard (optional)
400 g (13 oz) can mixed beans or kidney
  beans, drained and rinsed
1 red pepper, diced
100 g (3½ oz) broccoli, finely chopped
salt and freshly ground black pepper

Serves: 2

Preparation time: 10 minutes

Cooking time: 10 minutes

1 The evening before, heat 1 tablespoon of the oil in a frying pan over a medium heat, then fry the bacon and turkey until just golden and cooked through. The turkey will take about 3 minutes on each side. Drain on kitchen paper until cool, then dice.

2 In a large bowl, mix together the vinegar and mustard, if using, until well combined, then stir in the remaining oil. Season lightly and set aside.

3 Combine the beans, red pepper and broccoli and stir well. Add the bacon and turkey. Check the seasoning. Refrigerate overnight in airtight containers; stir in the dressing before packing. The second portion will keep for up to 3 days.

Chicken Rice Salad

Ingredients

4 chicken thighs, skinned and boned
175 g (6 oz) long grain rice
2 teaspoons lemon juice
2 tablespoons peanut butter (optional)
2 tablespoons oil
2 slices pineapple, peeled and chopped
1 red pepper, chopped
75 g (3 oz) sugar snap peas, sliced
4 tablespoons peanuts (optional)
salt and freshly ground black pepper

Serves: 4

Preparation time: 10 minutes

Cooking time: about 15 minutes, plus cooling

CARBS   **VITAMIN C**

1 The evening before, place the chicken thighs in a steamer set over boiling water for 6–8 minutes until cooked through. Alternatively, simmer them in shallow water in a frying pan for 10 minutes. Remove from the steamer or pan and set aside to cool.

2 Meanwhile, bring a pan of salted water to the boil and cook the rice according to the packet instructions. Drain and rinse under cold water to cool the rice completely, then tip it into a large bowl.

3 To make the dressing, mix together the lemon juice, peanut butter, if using, salt and freshly ground black pepper until well combined, then whisk in the oil.

4 Dice the chicken thighs into bite-sized pieces and stir into the rice. Add the pineapple, red pepper, sugar snap peas and peanuts, if using. Remove a quarter of the mixture and place in an airtight container.

5 To complete the salad, pour three-quarters of the dressing over the 3 portions that are being eaten for dinner. Place the remaining dressing in an airtight container and refrigerate overnight along with the rice salad, to be combined in the morning.

Prawns with Fruity Salad

Ingredients

200 g (7 oz) bulgar wheat
50 g (2 oz) dried ready-to-eat apricots,
  chopped
75 g (3 oz) green seedless grapes, halved
4 leaves from a head of Chinese lettuce,
  chopped
250 g (8 oz) small Atlantic prawns,
  defrosted if frozen, and drained
2 teaspoons chopped coriander (optional)
4 tablespoons sunflower oil
1 tablespoon lemon juice
1 tablespoon poppy seeds
salt and freshly ground black pepper

Serves: 4

Preparation time: 15 minutes

Cooking time: 10 minutes

1 The evening before, put the bulgar wheat in a heatproof bowl and pour over sufficient boiling water just to cover. Set aside until the water has been absorbed.

2 If you want to give a fluffier finish to the bulgar wheat, transfer it to a steamer and steam for 5 minutes. Spread out on a plate to cool.

3 Stir the apricots and grapes into the bulgar wheat, along with the Chinese lettuce. Add the prawns and coriander, if using.

4 Mix together the sunflower oil, lemon juice and poppy seeds, and season well. Dress three-quarters of the salad for dinner. Place the remaining portion of salad and dressing in separate airtight containers and refrigerate overnight.

5 To assemble the lunchbox salad, put the reserved dressing in the bottom of a plastic container, and spoon over the salad. This is now ready for the dressing to be mixed through just before eating.

IRON

N-6 FATTY ACIDS

Spinach and Orange Salad

FOLATE   **VITAMIN C**

Ingredients

2 tablespoons peanuts (optional)
2 tablespoons pumpkin seeds
3 tablespoons sunflower oil
2 teaspoons red wine vinegar
1 orange, cut into small pieces
75 g (3 oz) baby leaf spinach
1/2 red onion, sliced
2 tablespoons dried cranberries
salt and freshly ground black pepper

Serves: 2

Preparation time: 15 minutes

Cooking time: 1 minute

1 The evening before, heat a frying pan and dry-fry the peanuts, if using, and pumpkin seeds over a medium heat for 1 minute, continuously stirring, until you can smell the aroma. When they are cool, pack into an airtight container.

2 Mix together the oil, vinegar, salt and pepper in a jar and shake well.

3 Divide the orange, spinach, onion and cranberries between 2 airtight containers. Refrigerate overnight along with the dressing; the second portion will keep for up to 3 days.

4 To assemble the salad, sprinkle the nuts and seeds over both portions of salad, then pour half the dressing over the lunchbox portion, saving the rest for the second portion.

Lentil and Bulgar Wheat Salad

All kinds of lentils are good for healthy bodies and a healthy mind, and they go beautifully with the bulgar wheat and vegetables in this recipe.

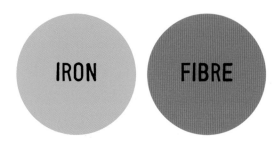

Ingredients

200 g (7 oz) bulgar wheat
4 tablespoons olive oil
1 tablespoon fresh lemon juice
1/2 cucumber, peeled, deseeded and chopped
200 g (7 oz) tomatoes, diced
2 tablespoons chopped flat leaf parsley
125 g (4 oz) runner beans, finely sliced
400 g (13 oz) can green lentils,
  drained and rinsed
salt and freshly ground black pepper

Serves: 4

Preparation time: 15 minutes

Cooking time: 10 minutes

1 The evening before, put the bulgar wheat in a heatproof bowl and pour over sufficient boiling water just to cover. Set aside until the water has been absorbed.

2 If you want to give a fluffier finish to the bulgar wheat, transfer it to a steamer and steam for 5 minutes. Spread out on a plate to cool.

3 Meanwhile, in the bottom of a large bowl, mix together the olive oil and lemon juice. Stir in the cucumber, tomatoes, parsley and runner beans, followed by the bulgar wheat. Lastly, gently stir in the green lentils so that they do not break up too much.

4 Check the seasoning and add salt and pepper if necessary. Enjoy 3 portions for dinner and pack the fourth into an airtight container and refrigerate overnight.

Rice Cube and Tofu Salad

Ingredients

600 ml (1 pint) water
150 g (5 oz) basmati rice (not easy-cook),
  unrinsed to retain its dust
1 tablespoon cornflour
25 g (1 oz) sesame seeds, toasted
300 g (10 oz) firm tofu, cut into bite-sized
  pieces
oil, for deep-frying
2 spring onions, sliced
50 g (2 oz) mangetouts, finely sliced
50 g (2 oz) bean sprouts
salt and freshly ground black pepper

For the dressing:
3 tablespoons vegetable oil
1 tablespoon sesame oil
1 garlic clove, crushed
1 tablespoon honey
1 tablespoon light soy sauce
salt and freshly ground black pepper

Serves: 4

Preparation time: 20 minutes, plus chilling

Cooking time: 15 minutes

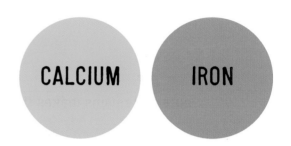

1 Take a plastic container measuring 15 x 20 x 2.5 cm (6 x 8 x 1 inch) and line with nonstick baking paper.

2 Boil the water and add the rice. Boil for 12 minutes until very soft. Drain well. Purée 5 tablespoons of the rice using a blender. Stir into the rest of the rice and spoon into the prepared container. Cover and weigh down with tin cans. Refrigerate.

3 Mix together the cornflour and sesame seeds and season. Coat the diced tofu in the cornflour mix. Fry the tofu in oil over a medium heat. Drain on kitchen paper. Refrigerate the tofu cubes in airtight containers overnight.

4 To assemble, mix together the spring onions, mangetouts and bean sprouts. Cut the rice into cubes and add these and the tofu. Mix the dressing ingredients and add. Refrigerate. Separate a portion for the lunchbox and pack.

Beef and Potato Salad

1 The evening before, combine the pesto, olive oil, vinegar and mustard, if using, in a large mixing bowl.

2 Add the cooked potatoes along with the tomatoes and cucumber. Check the seasoning and adjust if necessary.

3 Divide the salad between 2 airtight containers and either place the beef on top or pack it separately, according to taste. Refrigerate overnight; the second portion will keep for up to 2 days.

The addition of pesto is great for older girls who need a good iron intake. If your child is not a pesto fan, simply substitute extra olive oil.

Ingredients

2 teaspoons pesto, or to taste
2 tablespoons olive oil
1 tablespoon red wine vinegar
1 tablespoon Dijon mustard (optional)
200 g (7 oz) pre-cooked new potatoes, diced
6 cherry tomatoes, halved
1/2 cucumber, cut into large dice
125 g (4 oz) freshly sliced wafer-thin beef
salt and freshly ground black pepper

Serves: 2
Preparation time: 15 minutes

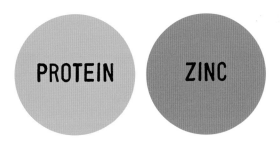

PROTEIN   ZINC

Honey-salmon and Potato Salad

Pre-cooked potatoes are always handy to have in the refrigerator. For this recipe, lightly cook a few extra beans the night before, or use frozen ones.

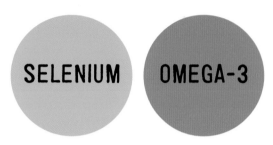

SELENIUM   OMEGA-3

Ingredients

250 g (8 oz) salmon fillet, skinned
1 tablespoon clear honey
1 tablespoon wholegrain Dijon mustard
150 g (5 oz) pre-cooked potatoes
50 g (2 oz) sliced and cooked green beans
100 g (3½ oz) cucumber, diced
salt and freshly ground black pepper

Serves: 2

Preparation time: 10 minutes

Cooking time: 15 minutes

1 The evening before, line a baking sheet with nonstick baking paper and put the salmon on top. Mix together the honey and mustard. Check the seasoning and add salt if needed and pepper to taste, then spoon half of the mixture over the salmon.

2 Bake in a preheated oven, 180°C (350°F), Gas Mark 4, for 15 minutes or until cooked through. Set aside on a plate to cool. When cool enough to handle, break into flakes.

3 Slice the potatoes and divide between 2 airtight containers, followed by the beans and cucumber and finally the salmon. Pour over the remaining honey and mustard mixture. Refrigerate overnight; the second portion will keep for up to 3 days.

Something More

Chickpea and Herb Salad

Chickpeas are a very nutritious food, low in fat and high in fibre. This tasty salad is packed full of good things and you can vary the ingredients by including your favourites or whatever you have to hand.

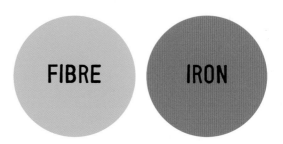

FIBRE   IRON

Ingredients

100 g (3½ oz) bulgar wheat
4 tablespoons olive oil
1 tablespoon lemon juice
2 tablespoons chopped flat leaf parsley
1 tablespoon chopped mint
400 g (13 oz) can chickpeas,
  drained and rinsed
125 g (4 oz) cherry tomatoes, halved
1 tablespoon chopped mild onion
100 g (3½ oz) cucumber, diced
150 g (5 oz) feta cheese, diced
salt and freshly ground black pepper

Serves: 4

Preparation time: 10 minutes

Cooking time: 10 minutes

1 The evening before, put the bulgar wheat in a heatproof bowl and pour over sufficient boiling water just to cover. Set aside until the water has been absorbed.

2 If you want to give a fluffier finish to the bulgar wheat, transfer it to a steamer and steam for 5 minutes. Spread out on a plate to cool.

3 In a large bowl, mix together the olive oil, lemon juice, parsley, mint and seasoning.

4 Add the chickpeas, tomatoes, onion, cucumber and bulgar wheat. Mix well and add the feta, stirring lightly to avoid breaking up the cheese.

5 Enjoy 3 portions for dinner and pack the fourth into an airtight container and refrigerate overnight.

Homemade Sausage Rolls

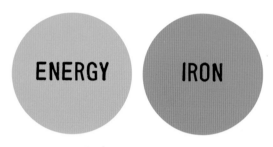

ENERGY   IRON

Ingredients

400 g (13 oz) of your favourite sausages
flour, for dusting
200 g (7 oz) plain flour
50 g (2 oz) wholemeal flour
pinch of salt
150 g (5 oz) hard sunflower margarine,
    chilled and diced
3 tablespoons iced water
1 tablespoon poppy seeds
1 egg, beaten

Makes: 24 sausage rolls

Preparation time: 15 minutes, plus chilling

Cooking time: 15 minutes

1 The evening before, snip each sausage at one end and squeeze the sausage meat out on to a chopping board lightly dusted with flour. Roll the sausage meat out into thinner sausages.

2 Sift both flours and the salt into a bowl. Add the margarine and rub in with the fingertips until the mixture resembles fine breadcrumbs. Add enough iced water to mix to a soft dough, then stir in the poppy seeds. Turn the dough out on to a lightly floured surface and knead briefly.

3 On a well-floured surface, roll the pastry out to a rectangle measuring 30 x 25 cm (12 x 10 inches) then cut into 10 cm (4 inch) wide strips. Lay the sausage meat down the centre of each strip. Brush 1 edge of each strip with beaten egg and roll over. Cut into 5 cm (2 inch) sausage rolls, or longer, and put on a baking sheet.

4 Make a couple of cuts in the top of each roll and brush with the remaining egg. Refrigerate for 15 minutes before baking in a preheated oven, 200°C (400°F), Gas Mark 6, for 15 minutes. Leave to cool before packing, allowing 3 sausage rolls per portion. Keep the remainder in the refrigerator for up to 3 days. (Alternatively, freeze the uncooked rolls on trays and bake from frozen when required, adding 5 minutes to the cooking time.)

Quiche Lorraine

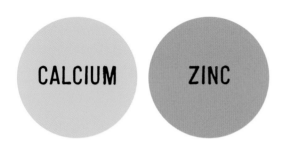

CALCIUM   ZINC

Ingredients

1 sheet from a 450 g (14½ oz) pack
  ready-rolled shortcrust pastry sheets
1 tablespoon oil
1 mild onion, sliced
100 ml (3½ fl oz) skimmed milk
75 g (3 oz) mild Cheddar cheese, grated
125 g (4 oz) honey roast ham, chopped
4 eggs, beaten
1 tomato, thinly sliced
salt and freshly ground black pepper

Serves: 8

Preparation time: 10 minutes, plus chilling

Cooking time: about 50 minutes

1 Unroll the pastry and use it to line a 25 cm (10 inch) loose-bottomed tart tin; trim the edges. Refrigerate for at least 15 minutes.

2 Heat the oil in a large frying pan over a medium heat and fry the onions until golden. Tip into a bowl and add the milk, cheese, ham and seasoning.

3 Remove the pastry case from the refrigerator and brush all over with some of the beaten egg. Add the rest of the egg to the filling mix and stir well. Pour into the pastry case.

4 Arrange the tomato slices over the top. Place the quiche on a heated baking sheet and bake in a preheated oven, 180°C (350°F), Gas Mark 4, for 40 minutes, or until set in the middle. Wait until cool before cutting into 8 slices.

5 Freeze 4 slices until needed. Wrap 1 slice for the lunchbox and enjoy the rest for dinner.

Spanish Tortilla

Potatoes are an excellent choice for children's packed lunches, giving a broad nutrition range with slow-release energy.

Ingredients

2 tablespoons olive oil
2 onions, sliced
1 garlic clove, crushed
500 g (1 lb) pre-cooked waxy potatoes, sliced
6 eggs, beaten
50 ml (2 fl oz) milk
200 g (7 oz) mild Cheddar cheese, grated
salt and freshly ground black pepper

Serves: 8
Preparation time: 10 minutes
Cooking time: 20–25 minutes

CALCIUM   VITAMIN A

1 The evening before, heat the olive oil in a large frying pan over a low heat and add the onions and garlic. Cook for 5 minutes until golden, then add the cooked potatoes and heat through.

2 Meanwhile, in a large bowl, beat together the eggs and milk, add the cheese and season lightly. Add the potatoes, onion and garlic to the egg mixture and stir well.

3 Heat the remaining oil in the pan then return the potato and egg mixture into the pan and cook over a low heat for 10 minutes, until cooked through. Shake the pan occasionally so that the underside doesn't stick too much. Use a wooden spoon to turn over the egg in the base of the pan, to allow the middle to cook through.

4 When the eggs have set, run a palette knife or fish slice underneath the tortilla to loosen it, remove the pan from the heat and put a plate over the top. Use an oven glove to turn the pan over to turn the tortilla out on to the plate. Slide the tortilla back into the pan and cook for a further 5 minutes. Turn out on to a plate and allow to cool.

5 Enjoy 3 slices for dinner and wrap the rest securely and refrigerate. Use 1 portion for the lunchbox next day, and eat the remainder for dinner/in a lunchbox within 3 days.

Falafel Skewers

Falafel, made from chickpeas, is tasty and healthy. Frying the balls in a good olive oil adds valuable nutrients as long as the oil is hot enough, and forms a crisp coating.

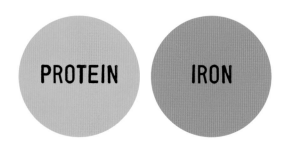

Ingredients

400 g (13 oz) can chickpeas,
  drained and rinsed
1 tablespoon water
100 g (3½ oz) cooked frozen peas
½ small onion, chopped
1 garlic clove, crushed
1 teaspoon ground cumin
1 tablespoon chopped fresh coriander
1 tablespoon flour
1 avocado, diced
2 tomatoes, diced
2 tablespoons chopped mint
1 tablespoon olive oil
salt and freshly ground black pepper
4 wholemeal pitta breads

Serves: 4

Preparation time: 15 minutes, plus chilling

Cooking time: 5 minutes

1 The evening before, blend together the chickpeas and water in a food processor until a thick paste is achieved. Add the peas, onion, garlic, cumin, coriander, flour and seasoning and blend again.

2 Use 2 spoons to shape the mixture into 8 balls on a plate. Flatten the top slightly and chill for 30 minutes to make firm. Place the avocado and tomato in a bowl, season and stir through the mint.

3 Heat the oil in a frying pan over a medium heat and fry the falafel balls until golden, about 5 minutes, turning once. Drain on kitchen paper.

4 Toast the pitta breads and slice into fingers. Thread 2 falafel balls on to a rounded white lollipop stick, with a piece of avocado and tomato, and repeat until all the balls are used up. Serve 3 portions for dinner with any remaining tomato and avocado and refrigerate the remaining skewer for the lunchbox.

Sweet Potato and Ham Burgers

CAROTENE VITAMIN C

Ingredients

500 g (1 lb) white potatoes, diced
200 g (7 oz) carrots, diced
200 g (7 oz) sweet potato, diced
25 g (1 oz) butter or sunflower margarine
2 garlic cloves, finely chopped
1 egg, beaten
250 g (8 oz) ham, chopped
salt and freshly ground black pepper

Makes: 12 burgers

Preparation time: 20 minutes

Cooking time: 30 minutes

1 The evening before, place the potatoes and carrots in a steamer and steam for 10 minutes, or until tender. Add the sweet potato after 5 minutes.

2 Meanwhile, melt the butter in a large frying pan over a medium heat and fry the garlic, making sure it doesn't turn brown. Set aside.

3 When the vegetables are cooked through, spoon into a large bowl. Add the garlic and butter, beaten egg, chopped ham and seasoning and mash well. Allow to cool before shaping into 12 burgers.

4 Line a baking sheet with nonstick baking paper and place the burgers on it. Bake in a preheated oven, 180°C (350°F), Gas Mark 4, for 20 minutes until golden and firm.

5 Serve 9 of the burgers (3 per serving) hot for dinner with baked beans or pasta in a tomato sauce. Leave the remainder to cool then wrap and refrigerate overnight.

Potato and Cheese Burgers

These great little potato burgers can be made for dinner and packed for lunch the next day.

Ingredients

750 g (1½ lb) red or waxy potatoes, unpeeled
200 g (7 oz) mild Cheddar cheese, grated
1 red onion, finely chopped
25 g (1 oz) butter
salt and freshly ground black pepper

Makes: 6 burgers

Preparation time: 10 minutes

Cooking time: 25 minutes

1 The evening before, put the potatoes in a large pan of water and bring to the boil. Boil for about 20 minutes until the potatoes are just cooked but firm. Drain and cool.

2 Peel the potatoes and grate them into a bowl. Stir in the grated cheese, chopped onion and seasoning. With wet hands shape into 6 rounds then press down with 2 fingers to form into burgers. Neaten up the edges.

3 Set a heavy-based frying pan over a medium heat and melt half the butter. Cook the burgers in 2 batches, using the remaining butter, until golden brown, which will take about 5 minutes, turning once. Set aside to cool.

4 Enjoy 4 burgers for dinner, served with lightly smoked trout fillets and cucumber slices, and pack the remaining burgers into an airtight container. Keep in the refrigerator for up to 3 days.

Cornbread Pissaladiere

Ingredients

4 tablespoons olive oil
1 kg (2 lb) mild Spanish onions, sliced
1 garlic clove, crushed
25 g (1 oz) can anchovies in oil, drained
(optional)
250 g (8 oz) cornmeal or fine polenta
1/2 teaspoon salt
1 teaspoon baking powder
1/2 teaspoon bicarbonate of soda
284 ml (10 fl oz) carton buttermilk
2 eggs, beaten
125 g (4 oz) sunflower margarine, melted
salt and freshly ground black pepper

Makes: 6 slices

Preparation time: 15 minutes

Cooking time: 55–60 minutes

1 The evening before, line a 35 x 25 cm (14 x 10 inch) baking sheet with nonstick baking paper.

2 Heat the olive oil over a medium heat in a large frying pan and add the onions and garlic. Cook for 30 minutes, stirring often. At the end of this time, taste and season lightly. Mash the anchovies, if using, and stir them in. Set aside.

3 Meanwhile, in a large bowl mix together the cornmeal, salt, baking powder and bicarbonate of soda. In a large jug combine the buttermilk, eggs and melted margarine. Make a well in the centre of the dry ingredients and stir in the egg mixture until well combined.

4 Press this mixture into the base of the baking sheet, and spoon the onions over the base.

5 Bake in a preheated oven, 200°C (400°F), Gas Mark 6, for 25–30 minutes until the dough is cooked through and slightly golden. Cool in the tin before cutting into 6 squares. Serve 4 slices for dinner and refrigerate the remaining 2 slices, wrapped securely, for 1–2 lunchboxes, depending on appetite.

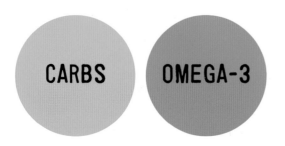

CARBS OMEGA-3

Curried Vegetable Samosas

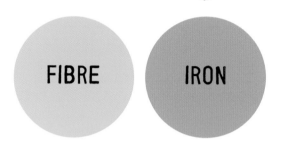

FIBRE

IRON

Ingredients

125 g (4 oz) frozen peas
1 tablespoon oil
1 small onion, chopped
1 tablespoon mild curry powder
75 g (3 oz) cooked potato, diced
1 tablespoon tomato purée
1 tomato, chopped
flour, for dusting
$^1/_2$ x 500 g (1 lb) pack shortcrust pastry
1 egg, beaten
$^1/_2$ teaspoon turmeric
2 tablespoons milk
salt and freshly ground black pepper

Makes: 12 samosas

Preparation time: 20 minutes

Cooking time: 25 minutes

1 Put the peas into a heatproof jug and pour over boiling water. Leave to stand for 5 minutes, then drain.

2 Cook the onion over a medium heat until soft. Stir in the curry powder, peas, potato, tomato purée and tomato. Season. Cook for 5 minutes, stirring often. Set aside.

3 On a floured surface roll out the pastry until it is 3 mm (⅛ inch) thick. Cut into 12 squares. Mix together the egg, turmeric and milk. Put a teaspoonful of filling in the centre of each square. Brush around the edges with the egg mixture and bring the corners over to meet, forming a triangle, pressing well all round. Brush all over with the egg mixture.

4 Put the samosas on a heated baking sheet and bake in a preheated oven, 200°C (400°F), Gas Mark 6, for 15 minutes. Wrap when cold and refrigerate overnight.

Potato Soup

On a cold winter's day there is nothing better than soup to turn up the inner thermostat, whether in a vacuum flask at lunchtime or as an after-school snack. This recipe is also great for filling-up hungry teenagers.

FIBRE   VITAMIN C

Ingredients

25 g (1 oz) butter
1 onion, roughly chopped
2 large potatoes, peeled and roughly chopped
1 bay leaf
300 ml (½ pint) chicken stock
salt and freshly ground black pepper

Serves: 2

Preparation time: 10 minutes

Cooking time: 20 minutes

1 The evening before for a lunchbox or during the day for an after-school snack, heat the butter in a medium-sized saucepan over a medium heat. Add the onions and cook for about 5 minutes until softened and a little golden.

2 Stir in the potatoes, bay leaf and chicken stock. Bring to a simmer and cook for about 15 minutes until the potatoes are cooked through.

3 Blend with a hand blender or food processor. Adjust the seasoning, if necessary.

4 Serve hot, or leave to go cold then refrigerate in a airtight container until the next day.

Tuna and Tomato Pasties

Ingredients

250 g (8 oz) plain flour
25 g (1 oz) wholemeal flour
pinch of salt
125 g (4 oz) hard sunflower margarine,
  chilled and diced
3 tablespoons iced water
flour, for dusting
2 x 150 g (5 oz) cans tuna steak in brine,
  drained
2 tomatoes, chopped
3 spring onions, finely chopped
1 egg, beaten
50 ml (2 fl oz) milk
salt and freshly ground black pepper

Makes: 6

Preparation time: 15 minutes, plus chilling

Cooking time: 30 minutes

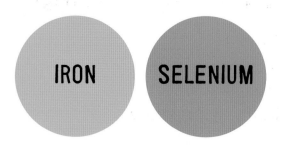

IRON   SELENIUM

1 Place the flours in a bowl with the salt and rub in the margarine until the mixture resembles fine breadcrumbs. Add enough cold water to mix to a soft dough. Turn the dough out on to a lightly floured surface and knead briefly.

2 Roll out the pastry to a thickness of 3 mm (⅛ inch). Cut circles out using a small plate as a guide. Reroll the dough as necessary to cut 6 circles. Rest the pastry for at least 15 minutes in the refrigerator.

3 In a bowl, mix together the tuna, tomatoes and spring onions. Season. Mix together the egg and milk.

4 Lay out the pastry circles on a floured work surface and spoon some filling in the centre of each. Brush all around the edge with some of the beaten egg mixture. Bring both sides up to the centre and crimp together neatly between forefinger and thumb. Refrigerate while you finish the batch. Brush all over with the egg mixture, if liked.

5 Put the pasties on a heated baking sheet and bake in a preheated oven, 200°C (400°F), Gas Mark 6, for 30 minutes until the pastry is cooked. Allow to cool to room temperature before wrapping in foil, or serve warm with a salad. Refrigerate for up to 3 days.

Green Pea, Mint and Feta Dip

CALCIUM **FOLATE**

Ingredients

200 g (7 oz) frozen peas
large sprig of mint
125 g (4 oz) feta cheese, drained and diced
3 spring onions, finely chopped
2 tablespoons lemon juice
2 tablespoons olive oil
75 g (3 oz) Greek yogurt
freshly ground black pepper

To serve:
pitta breads, lavash or chapattis, carrot sticks, celery sticks, red pepper sticks, cooked new potatoes and/or apple wedges

Serves: 6

Preparation time: 10 minutes, plus standing

Cooking time: 2 minutes

1 The evening before, mix together the peas and mint in a heatproof bowl, pour boiling water over them, leave to stand for 5 minutes then drain.

2 Combine the peas with the rest of the dip ingredients and purée either in a food processor or in a bowl using a hand-held blender. Check the seasoning.

3 Toast the flat breads and slice while still warm. Serve 4 portions of the dip with a selection of the suggested vegetables as an appetizer for dinner. Refrigerate the remaining 2 portions overnight, using 1 for the lunchbox and keeping the other for up to 3 days.

Chicken and Vegetable Skewers

These tasty skewers combine crunchy vegetables with honey-glazed chicken. For young children, substitute wooden skewers with rounded white lollipop sticks for safety.

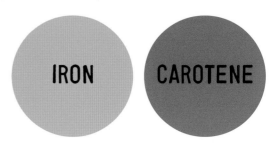

IRON   CAROTENE

Ingredients

4 chicken thighs, skinned and boned
2 tablespoons clear honey
2 tablespoons mild wholegrain mustard
1 courgette, cut into 8 large pieces
1 carrot, cut into 8 large pieces

Serves: 4

Preparation time: 10 minutes

Cooking time: 15 minutes

1 The evening before, cut the thighs into bite-sized pieces and toss in the honey and mustard.

2 Arrange the chicken pieces on a baking sheet and bake in a preheated oven, 180°C (350°F), Gas Mark 4, for 15 minutes until cooked through and lightly golden. Set aside and leave to cool.

3 Take 8 lollipop sticks or bamboo skewers and thread with the cooked chicken pieces and the vegetables. (If using lollipop sticks, you will need to pierce the chicken and vegetable pieces with a skewer first to make the holes.)

4 Enjoy 3 portions for dinner and refrigerate the remaining portion overnight in an airtight container. If packing into a lunchbox add a pot of the honey and mustard mixture for dipping.

Cheese Twists

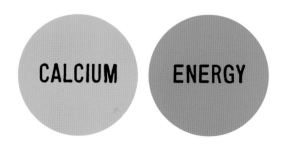

Ingredients

200 g (7 oz) plain flour
50 g (2 oz) wholemeal flour
125 g (4 oz) butter or hard sunflower
  margarine, chilled and diced
6 tablespoons iced water
4 tablespoons grated Parmesan cheese
3 tablespoons mixed seeds, toasted
flour, for dusting
1 egg, beaten
salt and freshly ground black pepper

Makes: 24 twists

Preparation time: 15 minutes, plus chilling

Cooking time: 15 minutes

1 Line a baking sheet with nonstick baking paper.

2 Place the flours in a bowl with a little salt, add the butter or margarine and rub in with the fingertips until the mixture resembles fine breadcrumbs. Slowly add enough water to mix to a soft dough. Stir in the grated Parmesan and seeds. Season.

3 Turn the dough out on to a lightly floured surface and knead briefly.

4 Roll out the dough to an even thickness of 3 mm (⅛ inch) or so. Cut into 2.5 cm (1 inch) wide strips, twist each one and lay on the baking sheet. Refrigerate for 20 minutes.

5 Brush with the beaten egg. Bake in a preheated oven, 200°C (400°F), Gas Mark 6, for 15 minutes until golden brown. Put on a wire rack to cool.

6 Serve 4 twists warm for an after-school snack and keep the remaining twists in an airtight container for a few days for use in lunchboxes or as snacks. Alternatively, freeze on a baking tray before transferring to bags and keeping in the freezer.

Mini Cheese Scones

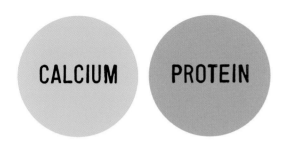

CALCIUM   PROTEIN

1 Line a baking sheet with nonstick baking paper.

2 Mix together the flours, salt, baking powder and mustard powder in a large bowl. Rub in the margarine until the mixture resembles fine breadcrumbs. Stir in the cheese then mix in the milk until a dough is formed.

3 Turn out on to a floured surface and knead lightly. Roll or press out to a thickness of 3.5 cm (1½ inches) and sprinkle with the extra cheese. Cut into little triangles, or use a cutter to make crinkled rounds.

4 Place on the lined baking sheet and bake in a preheated oven, 220°C (425°F), Gas Mark 7, for 10 minutes until golden brown. Enjoy warm for an after-school treat, and freeze any remaining scones for future lunchboxes.

Ingredients

125 g (4 oz) self-raising flour
125 g (4 oz) plain flour
pinch of salt
1 teaspoon baking powder
½ teaspoon mustard powder
50 g (2 oz) sunflower margarine, chilled
  and diced
100 g (3½ oz) finely grated mature Cheddar
  cheese, plus 2 tablespoons for sprinkling
100 ml (3½ fl oz) semi-skimmed milk
flour, for dusting

Makes: 18 scones

Preparation time: 10 minutes

Cooking time: 10 minutes

Not Too Sweet

Maple Syrup Flapjacks

Not only is maple syrup the most natural form of sweetener there is, it also avoids the sugar highs and lows of other sweeteners. Use regular porridge oats here rather than the jumbo kind.

ENERGY   VITAMIN E

Ingredients

200 g (7 oz) sunflower margarine
100 g (3½ oz) maple syrup
150 g (5 oz) soft light brown sugar
325 g (11 oz) porridge oats

Makes: 12 squares

Preparation time: 10 minutes

Cooking time: 25 minutes

1 Line a 16 x 25 x 3.5 cm (6½ x 10 x 1½ inch) baking tin with nonstick baking paper.

2 Melt the margarine in a saucepan over a medium heat. Stir in the maple syrup and sugar then simmer until the sugar is mostly dissolved. Remove from the heat and stir in the oats.

3 Spoon the mixture into the prepared tin and bake in a preheated oven, 180°C (350°F), Gas Mark 4, for 25 minutes. Allow to cool in the tin a little then cut into squares while the mixture is still warm.

4 Store in an airtight container for up to 5 days.

Peach and Cranberry Muffins

Ingredients

butter, for greasing (optional)
flour, for dusting (optional)
125 g (4 oz) dried peaches, chopped
75 g (3 oz) dried cranberries, chopped
250 g (8 oz) plain flour
50 g (2 oz) wholemeal flour
2 teaspoons baking powder
3 eggs
175 g (6 oz) golden caster sugar
pinch of salt
250 ml (8 fl oz) corn or sunflower oil

Makes: 12 muffins

Preparation time: 15 minutes

Cooking time: 25 minutes

1 Line a muffin tin with paper cases, or butter each hole then dust it with flour. Soak the dried peaches and cranberries in hot water to cover for 10 minutes.

2 Meanwhile, sift the flours and baking powder into a large bowl. Whisk the eggs, sugar, salt and oil together in a bowl until pale and fluffy. Add this to the flour and mix well together. Drain the dried fruit well then fold it in until evenly distributed.

3 Spoon the mixture into the muffin tin holes – about 1 heaped tablespoon per muffin.

4 Bake in a preheated oven, 180°C (350°F), Gas Mark 4, for 25 minutes until risen and golden. Leave to cool slightly in the tin then transfer to a wire rack to cool completely.

5 Store in an airtight container for up to 3 days or wrap individually and freeze for up to 1 month.

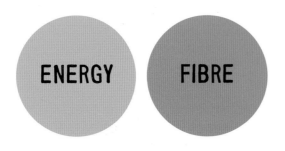

ENERGY   FIBRE

Apple and Berry Turnovers

FIBRE   POTASSIUM

Ingredients

250 g (8 oz) frozen blackberries or
  raspberries, defrosted and drained
1 tablespoon golden caster sugar
flour for dusting
$1/2$ x 425 g (14 oz) packet frozen
  ready-rolled puff pastry, defrosted
1 egg, beaten
2 dessert apples, thinly sliced

Makes: 8 turnovers

Preparation time: 10 minutes

Cooking time: 15 minutes

1 Place the berries in a bowl, add the caster
sugar and mix together.

2 Dust a clean work surface with flour and
unroll the pastry. Cut the pastry sheet into
8 squares and brush around the edges of each
piece with some of the beaten egg.

3 Spoon a few berries into the centre of each
piece and lay on a few slices of apple. Take
one corner of a square and bring it over to the
diagonal corner. Press lightly around the edges
of the triangle to seal.

4 Brush a little egg over the top. Transfer the
turnovers to a heated baking sheet and bake
in a preheated oven, 200°C (400°F), Gas Mark 6,
for 15 minutes, until golden brown and risen.

5 Transfer to a wire rack to cool. Keep in an
airtight container for up to 3 days in the
refrigerator or for up to 1 month in the freezer.

Oaty Banana Mini Muffins

These mini muffins are packed with goodness and provide an instant lift after school or as part of a packed lunch. If you don't have a mini muffin tin, this recipe will make a dozen normal-size muffins instead.

Ingredients

butter, for greasing (optional)
flour, for dusting (optional)
200 g (7 oz) plain flour
2 teaspoons baking powder
75 g (3 oz) porridge oats
3 eggs, beaten
175 g (6 oz) golden caster sugar
pinch of salt
250 ml (8 fl oz) corn or sunflower oil
2 medium, ripe bananas, chopped

Makes: 24 mini muffins

Preparation time: 10 minutes

Cooking time: 15 minutes

1 Line a mini muffin tin with paper cases, or butter each hole, then dust it with flour.

2 Sift the flour and baking powder into a large bowl and add the oats.

3 Beat together the eggs, sugar, salt and oil in another bowl until pale and fluffy, then add this to the flour mixture and stir until well mixed. Fold in the chopped bananas.

4 Spoon the mixture into the muffin tin holes, about 1 tablespoon per muffin. Bake in a preheated oven, 180°C (350°F), Gas Mark 4, for 15 minutes until risen and golden. Leave to cool slightly in the tin then transfer to a wire rack to cool completely.

5 Store in an airtight container for up to 3 days or wrap individually and freeze for up to 1 month.

Fruit Skewers with Yogurt Dip

This simple but effective idea should encourage your child to eat more fruit. Use lollipop sticks rather than skewers for younger children. These are widely available in kitchenware shops.

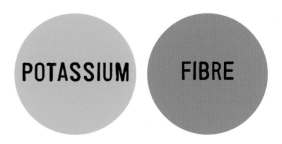

POTASSIUM   FIBRE

Ingredients

125 g (4 oz) seedless grapes
125 g (4 oz) strawberries
75 g (3 oz) pineapple, peeled and cut into
  large pieces
(alternatively, use blueberries, apples,
  mangoes, bananas and papayas)
125 g (4 oz) Greek yogurt
1 tablespoon wheatgerm
100 g (3½ oz) probiotic yogurt drink –
  flavour of your choice

Serves: 4

Preparation time: 5 minutes

1 Push a grape, a piece of pineapple and a strawberry on to a skewer or rounded lollipop stick. Continue until all the fruit is used up.

2 Mix together the Greek yogurt, wheatgerm and yogurt drink.

3 Serve 2 fruit sticks per lunchbox with a pot of the yogurt dip.

Choc-peanut Cake

Peanut butter is a good source of nutrition. If your school is a nut-free zone, simply leave it out – the result with be a moister texture and lighter.

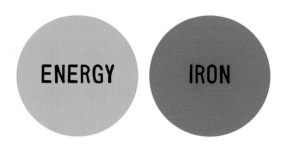

Ingredients

125 g (4 oz) plain flour
50 g (2 oz) wholemeal flour
1 teaspoon baking powder
3 tablespoons golden caster sugar
100 g (3½ oz) smooth peanut butter
125 g (4 oz) butter, softened
3 eggs, lightly beaten
1 teaspoon vanilla extract
50 ml (2 fl oz) apple juice
100 g (3½ oz) chocolate chips, or plain chocolate, chopped
1 large dessert apple, peeled and chopped

Makes: a 1 kg (2 lb) loaf cake

Preparation time: 15 minutes

Cooking time: 1 hour

1 Line a 1 kg (2 lb) loaf tin with nonstick baking paper.

2 Sift the flours and baking powder into a large bowl. Mix in the sugar, peanut butter, butter, eggs, vanilla extract and apple juice. Stir through the chocolate chips and apple.

3 Spoon the mixture into the prepared tin and bake in a preheated oven, 180°C (350°F), Gas Mark 4, for 1 hour. To see if it is cooked, insert a skewer in the centre of the loaf: if it comes out clean then it is done, but if cake mix is attached to the skewer it will need another 10 minutes.

4 Remove the cake from the oven and turn out on to a wire rack. Peel off the baking paper and leave to cool.

5 Store in an airtight container for up to 3 days or slice and wrap slices individually and freeze for up to 1 month.

Coconut and Macadamia Bars

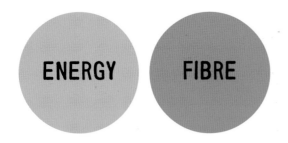

ENERGY   FIBRE

Ingredients

50 g (2 oz) desiccated coconut (optional)
175 g (6 oz) plain flour
75 g (3 oz) butter or sunflower margarine,
  chilled and diced
40 g (1½ oz) soft light brown sugar
50 g (2 oz) hazelnuts, ground
1 egg yolk
2 tablespoons water
300 g (10 oz) reduced-sugar strawberry jam
2 eggs
25 g (1 oz) golden caster sugar

Makes: 16 bars

Preparation time: 20 minutes

Cooking time: 30 minutes

1 Line the base of a 15 x 25 cm (6 x 10 inch) baking sheet with nonstick baking paper.

2 Pour boiling water over the desiccated coconut, if using, and leave to soak for 10 minutes.

3 In a food processor or large bowl rub together the flour and butter or margarine until it forms breadcrumbs, and stir in the soft light brown sugar. Add the hazelnuts. Mix the egg yolk with the water and stir in to form a dough.

4 Press the dough into the base of the tin. Mix together the jam, eggs and caster sugar in a bowl. Drain the desiccated coconut, if using, and add to the jam mix. Spoon or pour on to the shortbread base.

5 Bake in a preheated oven, 180°C (350°F), Gas Mark 4, for 30 minutes until the base is cooked. Remove and set aside to cool in the tin. When quite cool, cut into squares.

6 Store in an airtight container for up to 3 days or wrap individually and freeze for up to 1 month.

Fruit Shortbread

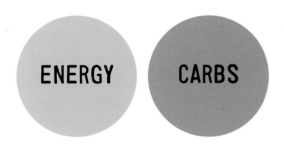

ENERGY   CARBS

1 Line a 20 cm (8 inch) square cake tin with nonstick baking paper.

2 Using a food processor or a large bowl and wooden spoon, mix together the flour and sugar. Rub in the butter, then stir in the almond extract and salt. Stir in the milk, until the mix just comes together.

3 Press half of the mix into the bottom of the tin. Spoon over the cherries or dried fruit before adding the remaining shortbread mix.

4 Bake in a preheated oven, 180°C (350°F), Gas Mark 4, for 30 minutes. The shortbread is cooked when a skewer comes out clean. Turn on to a wire rack to cool. Cut into 12 slices.

5 Store in an airtight container for up to 3 days or wrap individually and freeze for up to 1 month.

Ingredients

340 g (11½ oz) plain flour
125 g (4 oz) golden caster sugar
225 g (7½ oz) unsalted butter
½ teaspoon almond extract
pinch of salt
50 ml (2 fl oz) milk
425 g (14 oz) can cherries in juice, drained, or ready-to-eat dried fruit such as cranberries, papaya or apricots

Makes: 12 slices

Preparation time: 10 minutes

Cooking time: 30 minutes

Melon and Pineapple Salad

Melon is a refreshing fruit for lunch-time, and the cantaloupe melon is high in vitamin A, which is important for healthy growth.

Ingredients

½ cantaloupe melon, peeled, deseeded
 and diced
½ small pineapple, peeled and diced
grated rind of 1 lime
2 teaspoons fructose
lime slices, to decorate

Serves: 4

Preparation time: 10 minutes

1 Mix together the melon and pineapple in a bowl or plastic storage box.

2 Mix together the lime rind and fructose until well combined. Sprinkle this over the fruit and mix in well – in an hour or so the fructose will have dissolved. Decorate with the lime slices.

Date and Apple Muesli Slice

The only sugar in this recipe is in the dates – but you wouldn't know it from the taste! This very satisfying recipe is also suitable for diabetics.

Ingredients

125 g (4 oz) stoned dates
100 ml (3½ fl oz) weak black tea
250 g (8 oz) Swiss-style muesli
125 g (4 oz) butter, melted
1 sharp dessert apple, grated

Makes: 8 slices

Preparation time: 30 minutes

Cooking time: 40 minutes

1 Place the dates in a bowl, pour over the tea and leave to soak for 30 minutes.

2 Meanwhile, line a shallow 23 cm (9 inch) square tin with nonstick baking paper.

3 Mix together the muesli and butter in a bowl, then add the apple. When the dates are softened, purée them with a blender or mash them with a potato masher. Stir the dates into the muesli mix.

4 Spoon into the prepared tin and smooth over the top lightly.

5 Bake in a preheated oven, 180°C (350°F), Gas Mark 4, for 40 minutes until just cooked but still moist. Allow to cool slightly before cutting into 8 pieces, then leave to cool completely.

6 Store in an airtight container for up to 3 days (5 days in a refrigerator) or wrap individually and freeze for up to 1 month.

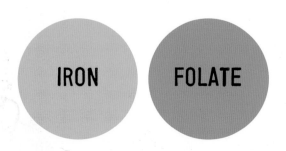

IRON   FOLATE

Orange Tea Loaf

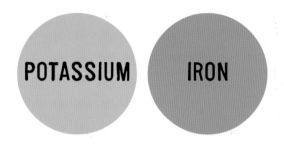

POTASSIUM　IRON

Ingredients

125 g (4 oz) raisins
50 ml (2 fl oz) weak black tea
2 oranges – grated rind of 1 and juice of 2
butter, for greasing
flour, for dusting
200 g (7 oz) plain flour
50 g (2 oz) wholemeal flour
1 teaspoon baking powder
$1/2$ teaspoon bicarbonate of soda
pinch of salt
50 g (2 oz) soft light brown sugar
1 egg, beaten

Makes: 8 slices

Preparation time: 10 minutes, plus
　overnight soaking

Cooking time: 60–80 minutes

1 Place the raisins in a bowl, add the tea, orange rind and orange juice, cover with a cloth and soak overnight.

2 Grease a 1 kg (2 lb) loaf tin with butter and dust it with flour, or line with nonstick baking paper. Sift the flours, baking powder, bicarbonate of soda and salt into a large bowl, add the sugar and mix together.

3 Make a well in the centre and add the soaked raisins and all their juices with the egg. Mix well.

4 Spoon into the prepared tin and place in the centre of a preheated oven, 180°C (350°F), Gas Mark 4, for 60–80 minutes. To see if it is cooked, insert a skewer in the centre of the loaf: if it comes out clean then it is done, but if cake mix is attached to the skewer leave it for 10 minutes and then test again. If it is browning on the top too quickly, lay a piece of foil loosely over the top.

5 When it is cooked through, turn out on to a rack to cool. Store at room temperature wrapped in foil for up to 3 days. To freeze, slice the whole cake, and put together back in the loaf shape with pieces of baking paper in between the slices, then freeze for up to 1 month.

Oaty Apple Pikelets

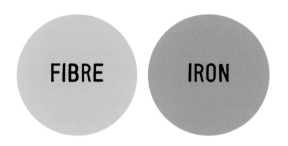

FIBRE

IRON

Ingredients

250 ml (8 fl oz) buttermilk
50 g (2 oz) oat bran
50 g (2 oz) plain flour
1 tablespoon soft light brown sugar
1 egg
1 dessert apple, peeled, cored and finely
  chopped
25 g (1 oz) unsalted butter

Makes: 12 pikelets

Preparation time: 5 minutes

Cooking time: 30 minutes

1 In a large bowl, mix together the buttermilk, oat bran, flour, sugar and egg. Stir in the chopped apple.

2 Heat a heavy-based pan over a low steady heat. Take the butter in a piece of kitchen towel and wipe a smear around the pan – if it sizzles gently when it hits the pan then the pan is at the perfect temperature.

3 Drop dessertspoonfuls of the mixture into the pan, spaced apart, and cook gently for 10 minutes, turning once. Repeat with the remaining mixture in 2 more batches. Set aside to cool.

4 Separate with pieces of nonstick baking paper, and store for up to 3 days in an airtight container in the refrigerator or up to 1 month in the freezer.

Malted Chocolate Milk

Malt extract is readily available from all health food shops and some good supermarkets. It is a great addition to milk drinks and adds vital nutrients to a treat. The almond essence gives this drink a nice sweetness, so you can add less sugar.

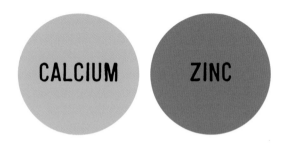

Ingredients

2 teaspoons cocoa powder
1 tablespoon instant malt drink (or to taste)
2 tablespoons boiling water
1 teaspoon soft light brown sugar
200 ml (7 fl oz) semi-skimmed milk
almond essence, to taste

Serves: 1

Preparation time: 5 minutes

1 The evening before, mix together the cocoa, malt drink, boiling water and sugar in a jug until it is all dissolved. Add the cold milk and stir well.

2 Add almond essence to taste then refrigerate overnight in a plastic bottle.

Fruit Smoothies

All of the recipes serve 2

Smoothies are easy to make and are great for treats or for an energy boost after school. Experiment with your child's favourite fruits to ring the changes.

Banana and Mango

Alphonso mangoes, the sweetest kind, are available most of the year. If they are unavailable, however, I would recommend using tinned and drained alphonso mangoes or mango juice.

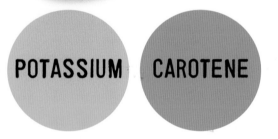

POTASSIUM   **CAROTENE**

Ingredients

1 alphonso mango, diced, or 100 g (3½ oz) drained canned mangoes or 75 ml (3 fl oz) mango juice
1 banana
100 ml (3½ fl oz) fresh apple juice
2 tablespoons fresh orange juice
rice milk (optional)

1 Blend together all the ingredients except the rice milk in a food processor or blender. You shouldn't need any extra sugar as the mangoes are very sweet.

2 For a longer drink, just add cold rice milk to taste.

Muesli and Raspberry

1 Blend together the muesli, raspberries and honey, using a food processor or hand blender.

2 Add the apple juice slowly until you reach the right consistency – the amount you need will depend on the kind of muesli used.

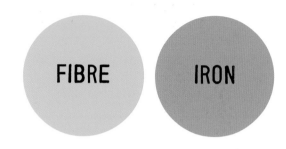

Ingredients

50 g (2 oz) Swiss-style muesli
75 g (3 oz) frozen raspberries, defrosted
1 tablespoon clear honey
100 ml (3½ fl oz) fresh apple juice

Strawberry and Vanilla Yogurt

1 Blend together the orange juice, apple juice and strawberries using a food processor or hand blender.

2 Add the yogurt and process just enough to blend, adding more apple juice if a thinner texture is required.

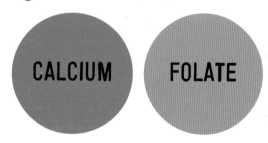

Ingredients

juice of ½ orange
125 ml (4 fl oz) fresh apple juice
75 g (3 oz) strawberries
200 g (7 oz) vanilla yogurt

Acknowledgements
Executive Editor Nicola Hill
Editor Emma Pattison
Executive Art Editor Penny Stock
Designer Geoff Borin
Stylist Liz Hippisley
Picture Library Assistant
Taura Riley
Senior Production Controller
Manjit Sihra

Special photography ©
Octopus Publishing Group
Limited/Lis Parsons

Other photography:
Octopus Publishing Group
Limited/Frank Adam 25; /William
Lingwood 29, 39, 43; /William
Reavell 33, 55, 63; /Ian Wallace 91.
Photodisc 71.

Ten Fat Sausages

This song is a firm favourite with the children I teach. It also involves subtraction, and counting down in twos. When you get to "pop", make a pop sound with your index finger inside your mouth. Clap your hands together for "bang".

Ten fat sausages sizzling in a pan,
One went pop and the other went bang.
Eight fat sausages sizzling in a pan,
One went pop and the other went bang.
Six fat sausages sizzling in a pan etc.

Ten Currant Buns

Children really enjoy acting out this song with someone being the shopkeeper and another person coming to buy the buns. You could also have real buns or cookies and some coins.

Ten currant buns in a baker's shop
Round and fat with a cherry on the top.
Along came [your child's name]
With a penny one day,
[He/she] bought a currant bun
And took it right away.
Nine currant buns etc.

Ten Green Bottles

You could use plastic bottles to follow the actions, or you could change the words to use teddy bears or other suitable objects.

Ten green bottles hanging on a wall,
Ten green bottles hanging on a wall,
And if one green bottle should accidentally fall,
There'll be nine green bottles hanging on the wall.
Nine green bottles hanging on a wall, etc.

Number songs and rhymes

These are an excellent way to reinforce numbers and number concepts because of the rhyming element and the actions, which act as a memory aid. They can be taught to children of any age.

Once I Caught A Fish Alive

This song reinforces the number sequence, and counting in ones. Count out the numbers on your fingers as you say them.

One, two, three, four, five,
Once I caught a fish alive.
Six, seven, eight, nine, ten;
Then I let him go again.
Why did you let him go?
Because he bit my finger so.
Which finger did he bite?
This little finger on my right.

One, Two, Buckle My Shoe

This song also counts in numerical order. You could count out the numbers on your fingers, and do some of the actions.

One, two, buckle my shoe,
Three, four, knock at the door,
Five, six, pick up sticks,
Seven, eight, lay them straight,
Nine, ten, a big fat hen.

1 Assemble a shop using the equipment listed, and involve your child. Ask what name she would like to give the shop. Write prices on the packages or prop them up on the foods. Choose prices that are less than 10 pence. Put each coin type into a separate container and ask your child to sort the rest. Finally, ask your child to write an "Open" and "Closed" sign, to be turned over when needed.

2 Decide who is to be the shopkeeper and who is to be the customer. Give the customer some money and the shopping basket.

3 Play at buying foods, using a simple exchange, with an item being bought for the exact money.

4 When your child is familiar with this, introduce simple addition. Start with a cost of 5 pence or less, and work up to 10 pence. Use the exact money, with no change.

5 Finally, when she has mastered this, introduce subtraction with a purchase that requires change.

Other activities to try

As well as food, include household items like soap, washing powder, toothpaste, shampoo etc.

Set up a clothes, shoe or bookshop. You could also try a post office, with stamps, letters and parcels to send.

This activity is ideal for when your child has friends around; it will keep them engaged for a good while.

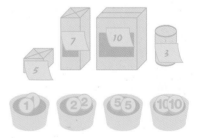

Tip box ■ This activity affords an excellent opportunity for extending language skills, so have some fun with it. If you are the shopkeeper, mention any special offers you may have today, say, "hello" and "goodbye" and encourage your customer to buy a new product. If you are the customer, comment on how lovely the shop looks, what tasty looking foods are on offer etc.

Introducing money

As a child I use to love "playing" at shops, and the children that I teach still love this activity. It gives them a realistic experience of addition and subtraction, as well as being a good introduction to the concept of money.

You will need

- Selection of fruit, packets of cereal etc.
- Cardboard or sticky labels
- Selection of coins
- Small containers to make a till or a toy till
- Shopping basket

1 Ask your child to carry the number rods to the table and to sit on your left. Ask her to build the number rods into a stair, leaving a space below.

2 Take out two rods and place them together. Ask your child to count the sections and discover the total. Remove the lowest number rod, and ask your child to count what is left. Do two more sums in this way, so that your child begins to see the processes involved.

3 When the fourth sum has been completed, repeat the steps but add questions such as, "We started with how many?", "Then we took away how many?" and "We were left with how many?" Finish by summarising. For example, "So five take away three leaves two."

4 Show your child how to record the sum on paper, explaining that this is how we write this sum. Do two more sums in this way, with you doing the recording for your child.

5 When your child is ready to record the sum, ask her to do it as she goes through the steps. Otherwise, she will forget the number that she started with, and the number she "took away".

Other activities to try

Write a minus (–) sign on a card and use the number cards from the previous activity to work through more sums.

When your child is confident with the number cards, introduce working sums written on paper.

Show your child addition and subtraction in everyday situations. For example, demonstrate with fruit, blocks, toys etc.

Subtraction under 10

Generally, children find the concept of subtraction easier to grasp than addition. For example, they often understand that if you have six apples and give three away, that there are three apples left. You might like to try this activity before the previous one.

Because your child will already be familiar with recording addition sums, both the quantity and the numerals are introduced at the same time in this activity.

You will need

- Number rods (Worksheet 1, and see pages 58–59)
- Plain paper
- Pencil

1 Lay out the number cards and number rods in order. Ask your child to choose a number rod and to place it on the table in front of her.

2 Ask your child to find the matching number card, and to place it under the number rod. Place the "+" card next to the selected number card, and explain that it means "plus".

3 Ask your child to select another number, and to place it after the plus sign. Place the "=" card after the second number, and explain that it is the sign for "equals".

4 Ask your child what she needs to do next, and she should tell you, "Count the numbers," or "Add them together." Help her to reach the answer using the number rods to count, if necessary.

5 When she reaches the answer, put it next to the equals sign. Do several more sums with your child until she is ready to make up her own sums.

Other activity to try

When your child is confident with the number cards, introduce working sums written on paper. She may also eventually like to write her own sums.

Addition using numerals

When your child has mastered the concept of addition with quantities (using number rods), introduce numerals. This activity uses the number cards used in previous activities to construct a sum. As your child progresses, introduce sums written on paper (see "Other activity to try").

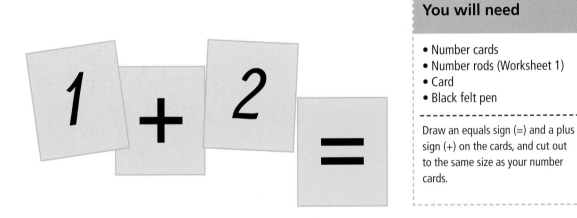

You will need

- Number cards
- Number rods (Worksheet 1)
- Card
- Black felt pen

Draw an equals sign (=) and a plus sign (+) on the cards, and cut out to the same size as your number cards.

1 rod, and to place it below the stair. Then ask her to find number rod 4 and put it next to the number 1. Select numbers under five, to keep it easy.

3 Ask her to count along the joined rods to see what number she gets. Make sure that your child uses a finger to count carefully each number rod section. When she gives the answer "five", explain that, "One plus four equals five." As you are saying this, point to the individual number rods.

4 Ask your child to put back the rods, and then do several more addition sums. Remember to use low numbers.

5 When your child understands the objective of the activity, tell her that she can make up her own sum. Ask her to choose two numbers, then ask her to tell you the sum. For example, "Five plus three equals . . ." You may need to explain the words "plus" and "equals" to her.

6 When she has finished the activity, review the steps that got her to her answer. Remind her that the number she finishes with must always be bigger than the two numbers that she started with.